VENERA

VENERA

POEMS

JAY ROGOFF

LOUISIANA STATE UNIVERSITY PRESS BATON ROUGE

Published by Louisiana State University Press
Copyright © 2014 by Jay Rogoff
All rights reserved
Manufactured in the United States of America
LSU Press Paperback Original
FIRST PRINTING

DESIGNER: *Mandy McDonald Scallan*
TYPEFACE: *Minion Pro*
PRINTER AND BINDER: *Maple Press*

Library of Congress Cataloging-in-Publication Data
Rogoff, Jay.
 [Poems. Selections]
 Venera : Poems / Jay Rogoff.
  pages cm
 "LSU Press Paperback Original"—T.p. verso.
 ISBN 978-0-8071-5429-8 (pbk. : alk. paper) — ISBN 978-0-8071-5430-4 (pdf) —ISBN 978-0-8071-5431-1 (epub) — ISBN 978-0-8071-5432-8 (mobi)
 I. Title.
 PS3568.O486V46 2014
 811'54—dc23
2013018693

The paper in this book meets the guidelines for permanence and durability of the Committee on Production Guidelines for Book Longevity of the Council on Library Resources. ∞

For Penny
who brought me to Ghent and elsewhere

Contents

1)
ONLY CHILD

Courtship at Isenheim 3
A Son For My Ex! 5
The Outer Banks 7
No Dream 8
The Kindergarten Heart 9
The Doors of Siena 11
Gingkos 12
Redemption Center 13
Practicing 15
Barbara 17
For Malcolm in Carolina 21
Night Light 22
The Porch 24
Adirondack Scenic 25
Butterfly Effect 26
Translations 27
Dazzle 28
Intercourse 29
Orienting 30
Mother and Child 31
Life Sentence 34
Dirty Linen 36
Only Child 37
Laughter 39

2)
VENERA

The Reader 45
The Mother 46
The Whore 47
The Light 48
The Window 49
The Daughter 50
The Door 51
The Vessel 52
The Virgin 53
The Sister 54
The Field 55
The Ark 56
The Queen 57
The Handmaid 58
The Soul 59
The House 60
The Earth 61
The Fountain 62
The Garden 63
The Singer 64
The Bride 65
The Mirror 66
The Table 67
The Lover 68

Acknowledgments 69

VENERA

1) Only Child

Every child is an only child.
—YIDDISH PROVERB

Courtship at Isenheim

About love
   no one said anything.
      Raising his hand from under
his wing
he raised her above
     all women. No wonder
        as she knelt
           in that heavy velvet gown,
             fallen hair flung down her shoulder, she felt
            let down

and turned her coloring cheek.
Her fluttering valves made her sneak
a look
    perfect for church
    had there been a church,
sly sabbath eyes nailing boys, not the book
       in her lap, where a virgin would conceive—
      who could believe
it?—a look
          she knew could kill.
          But an angel?

He was something, beautifully made.
Decked in gold brocade
    and red silks that swirled
       mysteriously around him, he kept his scepter
       back, kept her
at arm's length from his curled
        hair, his fingers
        articulate as a dancer's.
          In the red room
            the flint striking the steel chime
              of his bedchamber gaze
              ignited her desire to press
          his beestung lips to hers.

She would have died for that! but heard
   his sentence promise
      no angel,
         no man.
He gave his word.
            What could she say?
  How could she seduce
      heaven?
            She felt her heart
palpitate, her blood
    hurtle
  as like a torch his eyes
  sought her averted face.
            Her free,
   unnatural
        Ecce
          hid in its art
          her nerves' unbearable thought:
    an only son
  who would possess
   the only limbs to tangle
         with, the only heart to beat
     against her own.

A Son For My Ex!

When you breathed again your smile
on that greening urban hill
looked shocked as hell—
why did I whirl you and steal

that kiss? All afternoon in the dark bar
scotch chased with beer
had helped us deduce you from your bore
of a fiancé. Now bare

trees waved sticks blessing
us like lightning,
conducting us starstruck. Dancing,
your arched foot glancing

some fragile chandelier each time I'd lift,
breath held, hands on your hard flesh, I loved
you forever aloft.
Who could keep you? Left

for sheerer faces, darker plunges, the soul
evaporates like alcohol.
Flame licking my skin shrunk me in my small
hours, light licking the wall

and dying, leaden, the bed
enormous, no matter who shared
it, till one day waking re-glued
like a mug, I no longer knew you were mad,

no longer conceived our marital
chapter as ice-picked, hole-
pocked, inscrutable
as braille,

no longer wanted you in hell.
No jokes, no spell
or incantation that some vile
thing suckle you awake. No tail.

Well
in spite of all
I wish you and the baby well
in spite of all.

The Outer Banks

We walked out to watch the sun set
into the sound,
sinking sullen feet
into the sand.

The sun gleamed with a cooling flame
like memory,
like an apparition or dream.
You followed me

that twilight, late spring, sawgrass cutting
our chilled flesh;
wind whipped your hair forward, shrouding
your face.

Too cold! you said, turning to walk
back to the house
we'd rented, and I watched your back,
your thighs and Nikes

disappear. Orpheus.
In light like blood
I fought for breath while furies
or gulls said

nothing, hovering. The sun exploded
in a streak
over the sea; on shore I shouted
in the dark.

No Dream

My lips brushed it—or did I dream
that nape exhaling such perfume,
those fine hairs wicking it erect
in my breath's breeze to conduct
odors too thick, too sweet to swallow,
pregnant with roses and vanilla?
Did I know that softest skin,
a patch unsullied by the sun,
so smooth the fingers of the blind
would hush when knowledge reached its end?
How many groped that brailleless land
where breathless touch translates to sound?
How many watched you turning, deaf,
as if you'd known no human life,
as if you heard no drowning scream
as you sailed out the crowded room?

The Kindergarten Heart

Kindergarten heart,
   oh Judy May,
how have the blue years hurt
   you? Memory makes the downy
      hollow of your upper
         lip lovely as any form rubble
        shot from the mallet of a sculptor
       has left in marble.

I moved away. All moved away
those years where Judy May
   and Lynn Soffer
      sit sipping milk, eyes
      lit, mischievous,
        their woodblock fortresses
   guarding the future
     where their sighs
        betray me
  and offer
      love to men unworthy.

Their cascade of chatter can't hide
   the cynical curve
   of lip, the speculation of
      eyes that watch
the pudgy kid
   in drab olive,
      and bewitch
         him into a dream
  love
   will chrysalize and save
him, cracking to free him from the sad,
   balding, div-
       orced man he must become,

who sits in a room imagining
    their stares
at evening
        into their children's eyes
    and remembers
            when the kindergarten teacher
                Mrs. Silverman
        sat him in the corner after the kiss
    he still swears
            each awarded him when he handed each
                a handmade valentine.

The Doors of Siena

Glimpsed off a chamber, down an alley, out of
a fragrant window, they open—onto what?
a garden, a plaid bedspread; the infinite
or nothing; a de Chirico perspective:
skewed columns with a shank of sharpened light,
a misremembered shortcut
rushing you *bang* into a locomotive.
Standing at ends of long hallways I've heard
through far doors slanting open—onto whom?—
a nothing, a rustle, a fleeting word
I thought I recognized, a stifled laugh—
and known why the Sienese would paint a room
you'd pace as if blindfolded on a cliff.

Gingkos

The fallen gingko
leaves lit the avenue
of left trees. Among a washed-out fall their yellow
    dazzled like a dance
        floor
    lit under lit-up couples
        far

under the unruffled bare gingkos
and steel skies
    decorous above
that yellow shocking as a bit plum's bloodiness
        to a young girl.
    The gold leaf-
        fall

would cushion
    our step
smoothing our strewn
    way. Why couldn't we stop

our path's diverging, the dance
    rent to prowl
narrow pavements
        singly toward bars or embraces,
            to root in exotic
        aromas, locked rooms, dark houses,
            all while those local
        immigrants the domestic
      gingkos
              spread
            their brilliant bed
          their hospitable
    fall?

Redemption Center

Flying home, high over
    dreaming states, hurtling through cloud
        I shut my eyes and stand
        in air-conditioned
weather beyond weather,
my beautiful young mother and father
        on each side, squeezing either hand
    of their little boy. We glided
down dazzling aisles and I saw leather
    in the mind of God—

a Mickey Mantle–model glove.
    Heaven!
        But we hurtled past to offer
            our accounting: the dog-eared books
                infinite with stamps I'd lick and stick
                lick and stick
                long rainy days till my hands stuck
    to the walls and our walnut furniture:
            a shriek,
                and a hot washcloth scalding to the quick
            my gummy fingers. But immaculate clerks
now tallied and forgave
smiled and forgave
    and handed us a toaster oven,
            a miracle
    no one on earth had seen before.

Shut years ago—a shell
    smashed, gutted, its Muzak strings
        mute. Once a thousand stamp books' wings
            glittered gold-green plumage
        on every fluttering page.
Long fledged. A naked mansion, an urban hell.

As we descend
   my dream
      of the lost center cracks open. I'm middle-
         aged with parents
in the ground.
   Can we redeem
        nothing we love?
        5
    Cents
   says the empty bottle
in my hand.

Practicing

Debussy at dusk.
   When her fingers press
music through twilight like the musk
   of peonies
      I smell
   a place
   where the risk of a kiss
      once dragged her through hell.

At a seventh in Chopin drops
   start
      in her eyes,
   start
      drizzling
      onto her practicing
hands. She stops.
   I think she's thinking about her ex
   practicing across town. I fear she's

far
   from contracting
     their decade
     into a prelude,
       compressing it like a concertina
   and extracting
the air,
      squeezing
      it into something
    finely
   varnished.

Instead
    at the piano she opens the box
        releasing
            her demon
        into the dusk, closing
        with it, forcing
    the ox-
        ygen
        back in
            its dusty chambers,
    rehearsing
with each chord
the hard
            shadow he cast in that room
              brilliantly lit
              one night,
the voice that told
        her *Go on.*

Her damp glance
    catching and releasing
        me *(exhale),*
her hands
        day by day know their skill,
            recovering
            her fingering,
        foot firm on the loud pedal,
    practicing.

Barbara

In a barbaric world
    child against father
a grisly world
    refusing all color
the good
      townspeople manifest
an intense civic pride
      fixed
    on their rising tower.
Can good

come stone
by stone?
    The stonecutters who hack
    rock
      the quarriers have quarried
      and carriers have carried
by trestle or trundled by barrow; the crane
operator who with his fabulous engine
      raises
towards white heaven
      these monstrous
    precision-cut opaque
      jewels
      so the masons might set them lightly mortared
    ever higher; the architect
      whose limitless
vision
      makes him squint as he stares
into the sun;
even the fine gentlewomen
    come to gawk at the work
and gasp at the profane
      babble
      of men at manual labor—all revel

                in this shared belief
        in the pride
of the town,
    in rock
and its redemption,
    in its Gothic
                potential
            its promise
                    its life.

Amid all the hubbub
she sits the hub
    of industry
    the *primum mobile*
    of the economy
    of this town fixed on blank sky.
        Among this populace gazing up
        she studies the book in her lap
            a rare girl
            who likes to read whose single-
            mindedness can blot the cruel
                eclipse of reason like a tower
ob-
                scuring the sun.
Her robe
            blankets her hill
                unfurling in every direction.
            The town has devoted the tower,
                all broken
            arches squat blocks and impossible
    tracery
                a gift from a grieving father,
                to her
                    this cracked
            jewel

                    refract-
                            ing a light
            crazed and invisible
                as air
                            a light that can penetrate
                    sacred stone
                    and inspire the heart-pure
                to kneel.
Such stub-
    bornness (her patrimony)
                        has set her in stone.
                    Resolute as stone
        the hollow of her upper lip

betrays not a tremble
    her eyelids not a flutter
        at the prospect
        of her high prospect
    removed from every creature
    (her sister; her brave terrier)
    hunger
            for dowry
            tracery
                    for lace, palm fronds
    for bouquet and everywhere
            a gray
                absence
            minutely detailed an obsessively exact
        disdain of color.
            What prospect
    for such a girl?
                What imaginary
bridegroom? What invisible
    candle to light her chamber
            with mystery?

    What dance
  to possess the wrecked
and serene foreigner
      raised among us our Barbara?

For Malcolm in Carolina

An only son
an only son
    sent a thousand miles
    from crack wars and street sales
    to wander where the mockingbird whistles
        and not the police,
        where instead of a jaundiced streetlamp there's
the moon,

south to paradise
    with tractors and machinery,
hulks and explosions
too beautiful, too filthy and dangerous
    to keep a seven-year-old away.
To say he's

got a home
in heaven or this poem—
    what comfort? He
        belongs where he can tell
            the mockingbird's mood each minute
                and stain
            his hands with grass and cowshit
                to wash off in the rain,
where he
        can ask on the telephone
    hard questions of his dad in a northern cell,
    whom he will someday see.

Night Light

Oil lamp glows
in the dark lone house
   reflected
      in a mirror
and two windows:
    four planets conjunct,
      bred into a small gala
        of light
        spilling out
    to where I stand, staining the perfected
       night

whose stars
are no mirrors
   but a struck conversation,
a centuries-
   late invitation
   from abroad, translation
     impossible,
       the tongue
     inaudible
       the host long
     still.

Which way home?
   The artificial
     lamp and its three
       shadows
   signal
conjunction: walls, room
     and bed where you, love, lie
       sleeping, descending through household space.
       Paradise
       overhead is

beckoning
    hourly, seductive with fire
and black hole. Standing
    in desire
        between stained and stainless worlds of fire
            I feel welcome
            in both and neither, home
            in that I have no home.

The Porch

Before we built the porch
the woods hammered the door.
Coming home we'd plunge
from poplars into the parlor

where the hand-me-down albino
upright slipping its grip
in the bass confounds the tuner,
where houseplants droop

and the jumbled silverware
can't find its way
home to the proper drawer
or, when put there, stay.

Pausing on the porch, our handmade
halfway house
from green rectitude
into homemade chaos,

we hear the cold trees mutter,
Those unpaid
bills . . . that unplumped sofa . . .
that warm, unmade bed. . . .

Loosening nail and splinter
off the strict porch boards, bless
these our wanderings into
bewildering wilderness.

Adirondack Scenic

The blue-hung clouds dangle, a wavering curtain
above the stage-flat lake, as though a show
were about to start—I have a good seat
on the cabin porch. Offstage a cardinal
rehearses, some birds tune up, and from the trees
a wood thrush flutes an air like Debussy.
Offstage the loon begins an aria—
a *long* note—carrying it out onto the water.
A *long* note, a *long* note—and then it laughs,
it can't recall if this is tragedy
or *opera buffa*. Back and forth it shuttles,
deciding, and before I can call you out
to catch the ending of the second act,
asbestos clouds ring down, and I run
inside, battered with the applauding rain.

Butterfly Effect
FOR ANNE DIGGORY

Enchanted on the painting's edge,
a butterfly punctuates the page
where marks of pigment aim to fasten
explosions of a world passing—
frozen faults, stalled waterfalls.
The painter fixes wilderness
securely as the clip's black spring
preventing the image from taking wing.
Meanwhile the wings of the live insect
waggle darkly to deflect
an inch of air. Oceans away
an ostrich shakes its plumes in snow
and ice caps swell the polar seas
as your lips brush my eyelashes.
Fastening here, fluttering there,
which wings tune the darkening air?
Chrome skeleton? Black gossamer?

Translations

Starts somewhere in a subcutaneous
shudder, somewhere beneath the heart,
gut feelings parsing into syllables
about as easily as I can translate

the chocolate warble of the hermit thrush
fluting through a gauze of trees
like blood through a pinprick or tears through ducts;
its trill erupts—*doutz brais e critz*—   You tussle

with German in the bedroom, courting the vampire's
heart, while I ransack our nervous
system. The birdsong charms its listeners,
striking us dumb. What is the meaning of this?

Dazzle

For such blue this dazzle
   what sacrifice? None
   too great, none.
      Let liars in public trust go free?
      All day.
         Saints tear
         singer and soothsayer?
            Wives
            and husbands strop knives
in the jealous sun?
            Out of our power. Our power
lies in dazzle,
     our responsibility

to such explosion
   as eyes' blue
   through
      my irising,
   through
         to the nerve,
            a perpetual
    losing
        of all
            but dazzle,
a flirtation
               with
               the perfumes of the palpable
          an embrace cruel as the grave,
             as strong as death,
                the sky in desire open
                upon
             the slow dazzle
     of this world, at once redeeming and reducing
   us two
             in consummate dazzle
        to full
   zero.

Intercourse

"You guys stayed up *talking* so late.
How come you *talk* so much?
Are you going to *talk* again tonight?"
My knee nudges

your knee; you tell your boy we're sorry,
we'll talk quieter.
He thinks a moment—that's okay
with him—and goes. You stare

at me like a schoolgirl, and we count
the possibilities:
1. Like kids in Wordsworth, he *meant*
it: talking. 2. He's

speaking euphemistically
to (a) prevent his blushing
at knowing what he wants to know,
(b) pretend our thrashing

about comes as a trick of the chaste
night air so he need not
know, or (c) act unembarrassed
at our blushing that

we know he knows. Such ceremony.
Knowledge is quickening,
delivering grief or joy
talking or fucking.

Orienting

Cold facts can drive you nuts, what's what, when's when,
late spring snow subverting what calendar
we keep beneath the garden's amorous trees,
collecting swiftly round our feet and—fragrant?
Oh! it's blossoms—smell their delirious drift.
And isn't our love like that? Isn't it
urgent as fragrant petals, cool, skin-soft,
fluttering down to pile up in our palms
but disappearing at a touch, huge flakes
melting as the sea embraces them?

Mother and Child

1

Hell of a place to start a family:
an abandoned building, a reek like a stable,
glittering with broken glass, rich with animal
filth, where a teenaged girl nurses her baby.
His lips clutch; she snugs him like a stuffed toy;
the remote father hangs, invisible.
A family? I love her impossible
imagination, her holy naiveté
here in the darkness. Around them fires bloom
where folks cook up their desperate sustenance—
how solemn their night progress to the heavens,
entered through a needle in the arm.
They kneel crystal with offerings, their waters
distilled in the effulgence of her face.

2

Bringing forth glory on her own without
wise doctors or shepherding midwives—the rubble,
the shining shards, a frightened girl in trouble
with one star dancing in the firmament
haloing her through a shattered casement,
a pickle jar for Jordan pot—Godawful,
simply undivine, unbearable,
a watermelon bursting through her cunt.
Instead of screaming she felt the world shout
(she cried for her bible); instead of blood
she sniffed a lack of sanitation, a primal
lack of grace. Still, she'd done it with her body
and smiled: no need of anyone! as night
engulfed the ruins. The child began to squall.

3

My antennae sniffing out this young woman,
I hereby declare my desire to nurture
and . . . love? I'd even change his diaper
as long as I might advertise as mine
that glowing, otherworldly flesh. Alone!
I'd shadow her into a leafy arbor,
hoarding the secret liquids of my ardor
rising in me in an eternal groan
like Apollo in his fever. If she turned
into a tree spreading her limbs, I'd abide
forever in the odors of her shade
descending aurorally about my face
and savor fruit instead of fruitlessness,
plucking the fatherhood for which I'd burned.

4

It might be malnutrition, but she swears
she hears an orchestra of fiddling angels
whose music she inhales, although it jangles
like hip-hop, like the dying fall that pours
in from the street, from boys in stolen cars.
She hears *him* snaking through the bass viols,
his determined intonation, his sinuous
chord smelling of violent death. Through tears
(it might be malnutrition) she can spy
only rainbows. Wait: a leg, a gold arm
now crystallizing, see those platinum wings
whooping it up, having a heavenly time—
how can she step in time, eternally?
Rising, she whirls her baby as they dance.

5

We're damned, exiled to kingdoms of earth,
given time to live in, given place,

given phlegm, bile, blood, sexual disease,
given air that won't sustain a breath.
He can expect an early, tragic death,
given gang wars, the greasy-palmed police,
beatitudes of crack: compared with these
the pains of birth erupted like a laugh.
Around her ignorant finger his fist has curled.
She's seized by joy. Death is impossible.
Nursing, nectar at her erect nipple
thrilling her, she trembles with the heavens,
and like all teenaged mothers she believes
the baby at her breast will save the world.

Life Sentence

At the bouquet of daffodils
from the prison greenhouse
   nurtured and gathered
      lovingly
   by the hands of a killer
      with Harley
tattoos,
hands that caress

the stems—as the guard
   marveling over his shoulder
   at his work has never
dared
      even in dream touch his own wife—
         and then quickly coolly cut
      their green life
         out like a light
   like a lover

her look—
   sun burst from cloud,
   liquid
      fire you couldn't get
      even if you put
         all those blossoms in a blender—
somehow her look
took
      its light
      from the cut
flowers, a look
      that under-

stood
only the body
    in its volatile
        cells can create the nerve-
        shimmering wave
    we love to lie about and call
soul,
    love
        giving no reprieve
        no escape save

the daily
dalli-
    ance, the descent
        into the bouquet of fire where we give
        off
    all heat
    all light.

Dirty Linen

In your absence everything
    inhabits your scent:
empty coffee cup, sandwich, paper and ink,
    all redolent

as the nylon, rayon, cotton
    scattered when you unsheathe,
the pattern
       of their fall
          a deciduous riot,
    rhythms of smell
        rank as air sculpted by Sappho or Wyatt—
there's a man I really believe's in heaven,
      when her loose gown from her shoulders did fall—
    head spins to breathe.

Nerves flirt with overload
    till to inhale
one more charged
    molecule,
        one part more per mil-
        lion could kill—

Yet good is the life ending faithfully:
    to have all matter knock
with your olfactory
    hallucination, and public
    moments veiled with the pungent shock
of privacy.

Only Child

A small child is standing at the bed.
That's what you said,
    that's what you're saying as I shake
      off the shock
         of your voice
      rocking me awake;
        then your eyes

open
    and you chant this text:
      Can you remember what I said?
      Can you remember— —You said
      A small child is standing at the bed.
    —Before that, before I woke. I think I asked
Who are you? What's your name? Who are you? —And then?
—I can't remember what will happen
    next.

Something
awful, something
    terrible.
       That's why I wake. —Something to the child?
   —I can't remember.
      Hold

me.
    You breathe deep, talk of your daughter
off at school, your boy
    off with his father.
      Imagine:
    the only child to get you up at night for water
      is the small child of this visitation—
        voice jingling
          like smashed glass, hand dangling
    an eyeless bear—

     our child. I cradle you, your back
     and bottom sweating in the dark.
  We breathe together,
     and the dark at my back
cradles me.

Laughter

> They resolved to invite to Florence the best craftsmen in Italy to make in competition, as a trial specimen of their work, a scene in bronze.... For the subject, they chose Abraham sacrificing Isaac, considering that this would test the competitors in all the problems of their craft....
> —GIORGIO VASARI, *Lives of the Artists*

1

Anyone can model men from mud.
Make them better! Cast in bronze relief
to make us gasp and cast out disbelief—
in what? Is it incredible, a God
demanding child abuse? *infanticide?*
suffusing his concoction—flesh—with love
so faulty it flees at the drop of a knife,
its bronze clattering down the mountainside?
Well, *can you do it?* Entries must include
one ass, one fat ram anxious to dissolve
into a thicket, two slaves goofing off,
and popping like a rocket from a cloud
one punctual angel with a timeless shout,
zeroing on that bright glint at the throat.

2

Maybe any birth's miraculous
but if your husband wined and dined a stranger
billing himself as heaven's messenger
annunciating your new fruitfulness—
yes, you, enduring second menopause!—
so what if he ate with unearthly hunger,
turning your cakes and venison to ether,
your wine to air, your kid to sacrifice?
You'd laugh too. And such laughter! a music
ringing down centuries, preserved in books
like wedding roses, like a butterfly,

a dry, sly rustle snickering, a goy
in synagogue, the unbelieving smirk
of Ravenna churches, those shocked mosaics.

3

The angel gestures toward the ram. The son's
bound body torques up from the pyre, his eyes
nudging the angel's hand. The servants discuss
the happy ram, the donkey thoughtfully listens,
and a lizard, crawled from under the bronze
gleam of a stone, reflects. Even the father's
old cloak, flinging a threadbare corner, swears
that on a nearby cliff the ram sits and suns,
an obvious solution, overlooked
only by the old man, his forearm cocked,
knife mindless as a compass needle, his bent
body scything away from the quadruped
and toward the bleating boy, two souls prepared
for the bleak relief of disappointment.

4

And now the boy's become an animal.
Hear how he squeals! But you'd squeal too, arms bound
behind your back, your trussed joints swiftly browned
over the laughing flame heating the marble
altar to a shimmer. Your father's arms cradle
your dark head—inhaling, you almost swooned
beneath the caress of his hardened hand,
slithering awake as from a tonsil-
lectomy. Damn his passion for instructions!—
rigid as a falling campanile,
his stern robe descending in tiers. Your shrieks
fly to his ear, buzzing their sweet corrections.
He's deaf as bronze. Sometimes it takes an angel,
someone to grab an arm; whatever works.

5

Funny how it all happens in time's nick,
ticked on a fallen watch. We should have guessed
the kid's gizzard had to escape unsliced:
in a frieze on the altar hot as love's nook,
our superpatriarch redeems the tyke.
My hero, cries mama. Hands unclutch her breast
to take the erect bouquet. We are blessed,
and our grapevines hang weary with good luck.
Bronze seduces us to believe permanent
say, those absurd shoes that carried our first
steps, bookends for mother's family bible
through which our hero's boy lugs his bronzed moment
when, like cider laughing from an apple,
the spirit from his body could have burst.

6

How much richer, my life before the angel.
One time we hiked, and he knelt on the mountain;
I hadn't known a man might kill his son,
and I tried to laugh. Flames lapped like the spaniel
mother swore we couldn't afford. The tickle
of his bronze blade, excited in the sun,
stropped on my neck! If only he'd not seen
the ram. Years later, that rank smell of rough wool
made me weep for that knife, those wings, the tears
of joy my father misinterpreted.
Blindly I blessed my son, my heel, who thought
he'd snookered me. Ha! Selling soup to Stupid!
Soup! So light, dark, it all boils down to bless,
curse. What angel ever dealt with that?

7

The story ends happily. All survive
save the ignorant ram, white as a Hindu's

widow, scratching himself, oblivious.
The servants stop in midgossip. They knife
thorns from soles, and wonder if the stream's safe
to drink. The lizard flicks his tongue and crawls
back under his rock. The angel hustles
home, bolting his door. How can people live?
The father brings the son home to the wife
and over mutton stew they share a laugh.
The old man, passing on his old belief,
dies leaving the son to confound his own
twin sons, hopelessly blessing the wrong one,
life bumbling on in comparative relief.

2)

Venera

How sholde any cherye
 Be withoute stoon?
And how sholde any dove
 Be withoute boon?

How sholde any brere
 Be withoute rinde?
How sholde I love my lemman
 Withoute longinge?

The Reader

So many distractions!—the angels crooning
next door, the organ throbbing down the hall,
out on the Sheep Meadow where she likes to stroll
crowds demonstrating at the fountain, chiming
like crystal. She's tuned out the singing, the groaning
virginal, the shouting colors of the parade,
and the jeweled gravity of her brocade
hangs on her like air. What can she be reading?
She happens to turn, happens as she turns
the page an old hand chances to have written,
her index finger marking what must happen.
Lips parted—chanting or astonished—she
happens to read the one book whose one story
chances inevitably to be hers.

The Mother

Not my mother, certainly, not any-
body's mother, yet despite the down-
cast glance, her face glows—that serene playground
look you see on young moms in the city:
engrossed in bestseller lust, but if some bully
tries to nail her lamb, her clear, alert skin
will hum brave as an apple, and struck blind
by love the little thug will slink away.
Such wide-set knees could magnetize a lover
marking beneath her gown a field of power.
Enthroned as on a birth chair, she delivers
us with one push into the universe,
rays of light loosed from her loose-shaken hair—
oh my, my children's, everybody's mother.

The Whore

Behold the painted woman on her throne,
my madonna of the patient thighs
whose book, transfiguring her loneliness,
tells tales of angels breathing on the phone,
falling to weightless knees with a heavenly groan.
If only they wore flesh for underclothes,
those off-key choirboy-toys. Sighing seductress,
bone-sick apotheosis of the bone,
if I could prime under your oily glazes
till your book smacked the floor, I'd wring a cry
from your high throat. Throw off your diadem.
Apprentice me beneath your jeweled hem
to labor in profound, unpainted places
I can't get free. But I would pay, and pay.

The Light

The gold light's created in the east trees,
abrupt against trunks, lovely in the limbs
looming like X-ray bones. In these rooms
new light makes everything antique—the brass
bed, oak dresser, last night's whisky—suffuses
the rediscovered world like gilt combs
combing gold hair, winnowing from my dreams
streaks of sheer light whose falling mess of rays
eliminates the need for clothes. White light
at day's height batters us from far above
the trees, wanting nothing to do with skin's
effusions or healthy glow, but like night
indifferent to the colors of my love,
the gold light that dances around her bones.

The Window

On one side of the window lives the world,
on the other the word. Her articulate
heat permeates the gloom, kindling my sight
till it flames like a movie frame stalled
in the projector. Alas, my poor world, charred
past repair! Let it fall to her maidish fate,
yes, she does windows, millennia of soot
redeemed on long hair, just a smidge of nard;
then with her lips she'll seal the brittle glass,
annealed by syllables that radiate
their glow through layers translucent as her skin.
If ink on paper glittered like her glazes,
I'd wrestle down opaque words to create
a stained world as transparent as our own.

The Daughter

I fall in love too easily with daughters
who've got this thing for Daddy. Subtle Barbara
sprawls meditative as a saint—her tower
in mid-erection, Papa's hundred workers
grunting—reading her book. Astride the tractor's
fender, my first wife chattered to her somber
father. The haying kept her happier
than wading at the Cape, quaint towns in Flanders,
the altar's sworn embrace, the nuptial bed.
Cut out the squawking. Here's one more beauty hung
up on Pop, hovering like a hawk over
his princess, talons out for any lover
who flashes like a falcon on her string,
homing to that heart kept chaste for Dad.

The Door

Either a door is swinging or it's still;
it's open or it's shut. I can imbibe
aromas, I can hear an angel sob—
me, moaning in poor prayer as I kneel
holding my breath, beholding through the keyhole
no Degas glimpse of her astride the tub
but full-spread thighs beneath her velvet robe.
Haven't I given you my naked soul?
Open to me my perfect one, my dove.
The ushers have removed the last drunk guest.
Feel your heart buck against mine as we clutch—
Hey! Open up! Clocks are striking, let's thrust
the bolt aside, our fingers dripping flavor.
I stand ready, hand trembling on the latch.

The Vessel

It's hard to conceive. I'm conducting research:
the leading candidates are cosmic rays,
some word raking hell through the universe,
a magic seed, or, in the joke a drunk French
priest once told me, "C'était le pigeon, Joseph."
Picture it in a flask, like the old Pyrex
stomach where Rolaids used to neutralize
our belly's sins. It's not the clearest image,
this cockeyed gnostic gynecology.
Still, her carriage in that heavy crown and dress,
the oceanic patience in her face,
and the calm finger that holds off for later
her book's climax, which she knows she'll get to,
confide her love can bear the world and me.

The Virgin

Her back turned on his primal nakedness,
her downcast eyes defy the gaze of the naked
woman, a fallen version of herself naked.
She reads aloud to gilt her loneliness,
rose rising in her face, the syllables
clothed in her clear soprano as the body
with muscle, bone, and sphincter clothes a void,
in garments rich and pure as nakedness.
The midnight velvet of her gown redeems
her own untouchable, her own un-
imaginable nakedness—bare arms,
breasts, belly, maidenhood in a golden grove.
Forever in her cloth of honor's weave
a gold horse kneels, bearing its golden horn.

The Sister

In the Park marching, voices ringing, at stake
all vulnerable virtue, "No more!" they shout,
"No more martyred sisters! Take back the night!"
By day the tower rises and the lock-
smith labors. Some of the best will starve stuck
in penthouse keeps, some stumble in the street
where a knife at the throat cuts off debate.
Don't be oblivious. Put down that book.
And when the dance floor heats up, don't react;
keep cool, a phoenix—no smiles, no eye contact:
that de la Renta suit conceals a slasher.
"Hey, sister," whistles the construction worker.
"Is it a good book?" whispers the junk-bond broker.
How shall the world be saved, beloved sister?

The Field

But into what shall we beat our plowshares?
The grain strains skyward with the best of us,
but my love keeps its vigil in the furrows
where zygotes sprout in passion, where the source
suckles the jailbreaking seed, drunk with tears,
until, against the air, it joins the lace
lining the field's lips, only to shoot like rice
back earthward, raining on us in the mire's
embrace. So all aspiration recycles.
Love straitens us to drag us in the ditch,
one of the universe's dirty jokes
you wouldn't tell at the drunkenest party.
But it's our joke, our love that's rude and dirty,
and when my lady suffers an itch, I scratch.

The Ark

She's so well-built, so trim, that any wind blows
her gently. Despite the warped world, she weathers
the wickedness of pimps and undertakers,
steering by her constellated virtues
her living cargo through the roughest seas
to port, where she must fend off smirks of sailors
and smart remarks of salesmen; and she batters
them back simply by averting her gaze.
In the warm hold, hidden, the animals
smolder, steam wafting from their hides and nostrils,
spring coiling round them, long cooped up, kept chaste,
a rumbling as in the guts of the earth—
can she keep these beasts clean, mad with their fast,
this keen desire desiring to give birth?

The Queen

Smell the lilies and the columbine,
intoxicating rose, seductive lily
of the valley, come smell! Can't they die?
Must they suffer the hothouse of her crown,
the stars of her triumphant constellation,
these fresh-cut flowers trumpeting the sky,
woven into jewels, pearls, filigree,
the spoil of oysters and the bloodstained mine?
Well, she's a queen, our lady must exploit
her naked subjects to keep lushly dressed—
fair tribute to the fair. I swear by the First
Amendment to stand erect. The cheapest
whore is as worthy of rank worship. Yet
smell those flowers, the perfume at her throat!

The Handmaid

After traveling all day you'll arrive
half-dead, an inn where upstairs you'll discover
a bed so made you'd choose to sleep forever
or immortalize the shredding ache of love
as though such verging on climax were life.
You'll ask, "Who is the angel of this chamber?"
and hearing water poured into a laver
turn and be taken by her. How to save
her from these rooms, the dusty uniform
in which she curtsies now, how to transform
her—jewels! robes!—what words of veneration?
A kiss might lure her into bed, where you
might barter some cheap ring. Such dreams, my hero,
such velvet longings. Such imagination.

The Soul

Flesh creates language, launching empty air
through her svelte throat's muscular double reed,
tongue and teeth drumming it to crescendo
up over her lips' sensuous sculpture.
Her word shrinks my world to a sheer idea.
And flesh makes paint: bones and muscles grind
earth; a dollop of oil, some sweat, and I stand
in my round world with a flat paramour
wrecking my perspective, offering me
a book, a blessing, a piece of fruit, salvation,
as if the flesh I paint could make me spirit.
Clothes make men. The dance drives ecstasy.
No fire to her beauty without ignition,
no life without the bed, the people in it.

The House

The house is packed, stacked. Bodies assemble
to watch a ballerina in a hush
of music—make it Suzanne Farrell—push
sex skyward into an ethereal
realm. Here in the fourth balcony hearts tremble
at such elevation, her arabesque
rippling up through the dark while ushers blush
at the elongate angle of her ankle.
The Gothic architecture of her body
obliterates all sense of ours, its lame
excuses melting with its aches. My lady
is built like that, propped up by knees and elbows;
the shelter of her hair, her hearth call, "Dance."
Enter, and be danced to another home.

The Earth

Deep in a black hole see my bluest lady,
blue luminosity fixed like a jewel,
tilt 23° from vertical
the axis of her head, her upper body
and mind bent like a divining rod toward me,
allowing me latitude from pole to pole.
I hope no more than to play her footstool;
the curtains of her robe descending round me
bring night lit by aromas of the sea,
the harbors of a sunken continent
of her desire rotating hourly by our
jeweled movement. Why turn to lighter day?
Stay to rain on this mutable planet
nocturnal seed, oh nacreous seafarer.

The Fountain

All things flow from her. We know her tears
create the stinging sea, and when she sighs
the ferries founder and the porpoises
and whales can't focus on their own discourse
for the disturbance. These are the waters
of life, the bitter fluids fleeing her body's
perfection with such speed that when her piss
drills a road to the earth's center, all wars
suddenly cease and enemies tumble in.
Her flowings are the means by which we mourn
the dead, the living, and those never born,
for mystery is in her menstruation—
like manna her ministrations trickle
into wine I drink from a crystal bowl.

The Garden

The trials of being human, the terrible
things they do out of passion, behead you, lock
you in a high tower, fire arrows, break
your quick legs on a wheel—all for the rabble!
In the garden the martyrs make their noble
march with the touching outrage of the meek,
waving their palm fronds high in the air. Look!
They want to be trees! That promises fruitful
salvation: not to die, but to feel birdsongs
trembling your privacy green as Daphne's
changes. Whoever heard such strange branchings?
Dressed in green desire still my darling climbs
skyward, still reads, still sings her arias,
lovebirds and lovers wreathing in her limbs.

The Singer

Or else her voice is such an instrument
as wrings grimaces from a singing angel,
a robin's wrangle, not a nightingale,
carrying a tune, otherwise untrained,
an instrument of evening, a voice blunt
as wet leaves, the rotting odors of fall
and mourning, yet with such a strong fertile
call as makes rutting spring feel imminent.
Via those obstacles to melody—
her teeth, her tongue, her barely opened lips,
her mystic media conducting my strange
trek inside her voice—her notes, like Möbius strips,
bring forth themselves, each naked flowering tree
shedding fragrance over and over like song.

The Bride

Chasing my darling through the snow-lit trees
to a room in a realm where rain always rained,
I knelt outside, spying love through the blind
and fingering the pane, its cracked glass
splitting my view between dress and undress,
light breaking from skin emerging ungowned,
unblue, unvelveted, my sight unstained
save for that other between her and my eyes.
Imagine my shock, my severest charge
short-circuiting broad waking dreams of marriage
with wet lips full of syllables that spill
like flung neon through rain calling *Motel*,
a sign, like light cast out of her forehead,
how willingly she could be spirited.

The Mirror

If marriage as a mirror of our world
gives us the ardent pair, blood-red bedclothes
funkily fragrant, garden-lit windows,
wood clogs, a little terrier, what world
does *she* reflect? What message does the gold
leaf back of her translucent skin disclose?
Speculation spreads like a cellist's knees;
she's like no other, mirroring each mere word
she reads, so what she reflects is mystery.
I ache for her to apprehend me, perfected
in her jewels' white light stupid as a star,
or to swing her eyes suddenly up at me—
I'd enter their reflection, her deep mirror.
That's the world to live in, all in her head.

The Table

The angel is in love with her. He wants
to break his contract as the messenger.
He wants to speak for himself. But what terror
in choosing the dreck of human romance,
to feel wing-feathers scatter to the winds;
worse, to have to eat, to kneel at her altar,
he who's never so much as tasted water,
his airy gorge rising at those communions:
the bread not even bread but always tasting
like human flesh, the wine rich, disgusting
as blood. Yet he'd eat at her board, he'd grow
bones for her; if he could encounter her by
chance somewhere, a garden say, even he
might offer her some food, some fruit or something.

The Lover

Love lies, neither emotion nor disease
but a text the flesh hungers to decode,
demanding a translation into blood
and gilt. See how the book of everything lies
upon her lap, as open as her face
whose downcast eyes have passions to confide
to the page, turmoils that, objectified,
would straiten me if locked in her embrace.
Lift your luxurious eyes off that page.
Nothing there can save us from the ravage
of the skin's quick touch into bones—old themes
crumbling our entwined bodies downward grace-
lessly. What remains!—absorbed by your face
absorbed in your reading of these poems.

Acknowledgments

Many thanks to the editors of the following publications, in which most of these poems appeared previously, some in different form: *Abiko Quarterly:* "Adirondack Scenic"; *Agni:* "Life Sentence"; *Arch and Quiver:* "The Lover"; *Café Review:* "Redemption Center"; *Chelsea:* "Mother and Child" and "Translations"; *Confrontation:* "Practicing"; *Crazyhorse:* "Intercourse" and "The Mother"; *DoubleTake:* "The Reader"; *Formalist:* section 4 of "Mother and Child" (as "Mother and Child"); *Georgia Review:* "Dirty Linen"; *Hopkins Review:* "No Dream"; *The Journal:* "Courtship at Isenheim" and "The Singer"; *Kenyon Review:* "Dazzle," "Laughter," "The Light," "The Mirror," "The Outer Banks," and "The Table"; *Literary Imagination:* "The Fountain" and "The House"; *Manōa:* "Gingkos" and "A Son for My Ex!"; *Many Mountains Moving:* "The Field" and "The Soul"; *Margie:* "For Malcolm in Carolina"; *Marlboro Review:* "Adirondack Scenic" and "Orienting"; *Paris Review:* "The Bride," "The Queen," and "The Virgin"; *Partisan Review:* "The Vessel"; *Poetry London:* "The Earth"; *Poetry Northwest:* "The Kindergarten Heart"; *Poetry Review:* "The Daughter" and "The Window"; *Prairie Schooner:* "Butterfly Effect"; *Salmagundi:* "Only Child"; *Shenandoah:* "The Garden"; *Southern Humanities Review:* "The Doors of Siena"; *Southern Review:* "The Ark" and "Night Light"; *Zone 3:* "The Porch."

"The House" previously appeared in *The Art of Gravity.* Baton Rouge: Louisiana State University Press, 2011.

"The Door" appeared in *Seven Hundred Kisses: A Yellow Silk Book of Erotic Writing.* San Francisco: HarperOne, 1997.

"The Reader," "The Sister," and "The Fountain" appeared in *Venera* (Saratoga Springs, NY: Green Eye Press, 2001), a limited edition, handmade, and hand-set artist's book created by Kate Leavitt, with her four-color intaglio prints.

Sections 1, 4, and 5 of "Mother and Child" appeared (as "Mother and Child") in *Hope*, a National Visual Art and Poetry Exhibit, at the Peconic Gallery, Riverhead, New York, and the Rathbone Gallery, Albany, New York, and in the exhibition catalog. "The Reader" and "The Vessel" also appeared online at *Poetry Daily.* "Laughter" and "The Table" were reprinted in *Lake George Arts Project Literary Review;* "Adirondack Scenic" and "Translations" in *Library Bound: A Saratoga Anthology;* and "The Bride," "The Light," "The Mirror," "The Queen," "The Table," and "The Virgin" in *UnBottled.*

I am grateful to the MacDowell Colony and especially to the Corporation of

Yaddo for residencies during which I worked on many of these poems. The Janet Sloane/Alfred Z. Solomon Residency at Yaddo enabled me to write several key poems in the sequence *Venera*.

I also wish to thank Skidmore College's faculty development committee for its generous support.

The *Venera* sequence would not exist without Penny Jolly's inspiration and expertise. I am also indebted to the work of art historians Elisabeth Dhanens and Carol J. Purtle. For their encouragement and suggestions I owe thanks to Terry Diggory, Sandra Gilbert, Marilyn Hacker, Andrew Hudgins, B. D. Love, Amelia Rosner, and Steve Stern.

www.ingramcontent.com/pod-product-compliance
Lightning Source LLC
Chambersburg PA
CBHW030123170426
43198CB00009B/716